discover more
Marine Wildlife

Sea Invertebrates

Kaitlyn Salvatore

IN ASSOCIATION WITH

Published in 2025 by Britannica Educational Publishing (a trademark of Encyclopædia Britannica, Inc.) in association with The Rosen Publishing Group, Inc.
2544 Clinton Street, Buffalo, NY 14224

Copyright © 2025 by Encyclopædia Britannica, Inc. Britannica, Encyclopædia Britannica, and the Thistle logo are registered trademarks Encyclopædia Britannica, Inc. All rights reserved.

Rosen Publishing materials copyright © 2025 The Rosen Publishing Group, Inc. All rights reserved.

Distributed exclusively by Rosen Publishing.
To see additional Britannica Educational Publishing titles, go to rosenpublishing.com.

All rights reserved. No part of this book may be reproduced in any form without permission in writing from the publisher, except by a reviewer.

Editor: Brianna Propis
Book Design: Michael Flynn

Photo Credits: Cover Vojce/Shutterstock.com; (series background) Dai Yim/Shutterstock.com; p. 5 (top) Zety Akhzar/Shutterstock.com; p. 5 (bottom) Victor1153/Shutterstock.com; p. 6 Wirestock Creators/Shutterstock.com; p. 7 ChristopherRM/Shutterstock.com; p. 8 Stefano Bolognini/Shutterstock.com; p. 9 https://commons.wikimedia.org/wiki/File:Dumbo-hires.jpg; p. 10 Rich Carey/Shutterstock.com; p. 11 RLS Photo/Shutterstock.com; p. 12 ChameleonsEye/Shutterstock.com; p. 13 Henryp982/Shutterstock.com; p. 14 Barbara Ash/Shutterstock.com; p. 15 Irina Markova/Shutterstock.com; p. 16 cbpix/Shutterstock.com; p. 17 Vojce/Shutterstock.com; p. 18 NatureDiver/Shutterstock.com; p. 19 dvlcom - www.dvlcom.co.uk/Shutterstock.com; p. 20 marksn.media/Shutterstock.com; p. 21 makesushi1/Shutterstock.com; p. 22 Daryl Duda/Shutterstock.com; p. 23 Jolanta Wojcicka/Shutterstock.com; p. 24 Rheanna Brett/Shutterstock.com; p. 25 mastersky/Shutterstock.com; p. 26 Tatyana Domnicheva/Shutterstock.com; p. 27 Steve Bower/Shutterstock.com; p. 28 Vladimir Turkenich/Shutterstock.com.

Library of Congress Cataloging-in-Publication Data

Names: Salvatore, Kaitlyn, author.
Title: Sea invertebrates / Kaitlyn Salvatore.
Description: Buffalo : Britannica Educational Publishing, an imprint of
  Rosen Publishing, [2025] | Series: Discover more: marine wildlife |
  Includes index.
Identifiers: LCCN 2024027442 | ISBN 9781641903608 (library binding) | ISBN
  9781641903592 (paperback) | ISBN 9781641903615 (ebook)
Subjects: LCSH: Marine invertebrates--Juvenile literature.
Classification: LCC QL365.363 .S25 2025 | DDC 593--dc23/eng/20240708
LC record available at https://lccn.loc.gov/2024027442

Manufactured in the United States of America

Some of the images in this book illustrate individuals who are models. The depictions do not imply actual situations or events.

CPSIA Compliance Information: Batch #CWBRIT25. For further information contact Rosen Publishing at 1-800-237-9932.

Contents

Under the Sea 4

Eight-Armed Invertebrate 6

Soft-Bodied Jelly 10

Invertebrates in Reefs. 14

Flowery Animals .16

Hollow and Spiny Stars 18

Echinoderm Invertebrate 20

Soft-Bodied Sponge 22

Invertebrate with Claws 24

Why Are Invertebrates Important?. . . . 28

Glossary 30

For More Information 31

Index 32

Under the Sea

Do all animals have backbones? Nope! An invertebrate is an animal without a backbone. Animals with a backbone, such as humans, horses, and fish, are vertebrates. Some examples of invertebrates are worms, snails, and spiders. Invertebrates are found all over the world, and around 95 percent or more of Earth's animals are invertebrates! They come in a variety of shapes, sizes, and colors.

Invertebrates that live underwater are called sea invertebrates. There are many different species, or kinds, of sea invertebrates. Some have stinging tentacles or claws, and others have spiny or squishy skin. Sponges are a kind of sea invertebrate, and their bodies are very simple. They are made up of a mass of specialized cells. Others, like octopuses, have more complex bodies. Octopuses have three hearts and eight legs. They can camouflage—or change their skin color to match their surroundings.

Invertebrates have been on Earth for a long time! Scientists believe the first multicellular invertebrates appeared on Earth as far back as a billion years ago.

compare and contrast

How many different types of vertebrates do you know of? How about invertebrates? What similarities and differences between them can you think of?

Octopuses are known as one of the smartest animals around. They have shown their intelligence through behaviors such as using tools, memorization, and navigation.

Eight-Armed Invertebrate

Octopuses are part of a group of invertebrates called mollusks. Other mollusks include squid, clams, and oysters. There are about 300 species of octopuses, and they live in seas throughout the world. Octopuses are considered the smartest invertebrates.

Can you see the cuplike suckers on the tentacles? Tentacles are like long arms that help octopuses to feel, grasp, and move.

The largest type of octopus is called the giant Pacific octopus. It's bigger than a 6-foot-tall human being! The largest one ever found weighed 600 pounds (272 kg).

Octopuses have eight arms and soft, bag-like bodies with large eyes. Their long, slender arms can reach out in all directions. Each arm has two rows of cuplike suckers with great holding power.

Octopuses vary greatly in size. The smallest are only about 1 inch (2.5 cm) long, and the largest species grows to be about 110 pounds (50 kg) with a 16-foot (4.9 m) arm span.

Consider This
Octopuses have eight arms. How might that help them catch their food?

Depending on their surroundings or mood, octopuses can change the color of their skin. They can be gray, brown, pink, blue, green, or even an angry red if they are suddenly frightened.

An octopus usually crawls along the ocean bottom searching for food. Larger ones eat mainly crabs and lobsters. Octopuses are skillful hunters. The big ones may attack large **prey** such as sharks. If an octopus is in danger, it can shoot a jet of water out of its body. This moves the octopus backward very quickly. Some octopuses can also release a cloud of ink to confuse an enemy. The ink can also affect the attacker's senses. This makes it hard for the predator to track them. An octopus's soft body allows it to squeeze into extremely small places where **predators** can't reach it.

Can you spot the octopus in this photo? It's a master of disguise!

The dumbo octopus lives in the deepest waters of the ocean. Unlike many octopuses, the dumbo octopus doesn't have an ink sac because it rarely comes across any predators.

A female octopus lays her eggs under rocks or in holes. She guards the eggs for four to eight weeks. After hatching, the babies are carried away by the ocean currents for several weeks before returning to the coast.

WORD WISE
PREDATORS ARE ANIMALS THAT HUNT OTHER ANIMALS FOR FOOD. PREY ARE THE ANIMALS BEING HUNTED.

Soft-Bodied Jelly

Another kind of sea invertebrate is known for having no bones and a soft, jellylike body. This creature is called a jellyfish. Jellyfish are members of a group of animals called **cnidarians**. There are more than 200 species of jellyfish. They are found in all oceans. Most live near the surface of the water. Jellyfish have existed for hundreds of millions of years—even before dinosaurs roamed the planet!

Sea turtles enjoy snacking on jellyfish!

Lion's mane jellyfish use their tentacles as a trap for prey. They extend them outward and capture fish and other food.

A typical jellyfish is shaped like an unfolded umbrella. The top part is called the bell. Some jellyfish are barely big enough to be seen. Others are more than 6 feet (2 m) across. The largest jellyfish species is the lion's mane jellyfish. Its bell can grow to 8 feet (2.4 m) across, and its tentacles can grow more than 100 feet (30.5 m) long.

WORD WISE
CNIDARIANS ARE A LARGE GROUP OF AQUATIC ANIMALS THAT INCLUDE JELLYFISH, SEA ANEMONES, AND CORAL. THEY ARE CARNIVORES, OR MEAT-EATERS, AND PRODUCE STINGERS.

Jellyfish come in a variety of colors, including white, brown, pink, blue, maroon, and even see-through. Certain jellyfish are luminescent, which means they glow. Some jellyfish have eyes around the edge of their body. Their mouth and stomach are in the middle of the body. Jellyfish swim by contracting and expanding muscles on the underside of their body.

A jellyfish may have a few or many tentacles. Thin tentacles run around the edge of the body. Four or more larger tentacles hang down from the middle of the body, below the mouth. In some jellyfish, the tentacles are

Although they're fairly common and usually not deadly, make sure to immediately tell an adult if you're stung by a jellyfish! If you know you'll be swimming in waters that contain jellyfish, it may be helpful to wear a skin suit.

Sea wasps, a kind of box jelly, live mainly in the waters off northern Australia and in the Indo-Pacific Ocean. They can also be found near Hawaii, Florida, the Caribbean, and Puerto Rico. Be careful!

lined with stinging cells that make poison. The poison can stun small animals. The tentacles then pull these animals into the jellyfish's mouth. Most jellyfish eat tiny animals known as plankton.

Certain jellyfish can be very dangerous to humans. Even a small sting from the jellyfish called a sea wasp can kill a person within a few minutes. Jellyfish do not attack humans on purpose, however. Most people are stung after accidentally touching one.

Consider This
How are jellyfish and octopuses similar? How are they different?

Invertebrates in Reefs

Some invertebrates live in enormous colonies called reefs. The creatures that make reefs are called corals. Coral reefs are home to many other plants and animals too.

The body of a coral is called a polyp. A polyp attaches to a surface. Polyps can be 0.04 inch (1 mm) to 10 inches (25 cm) across. At the top of the polyp is the mouth. The mouth is surrounded by tentacles that paralyze prey and bring the prey into the mouth.

Many fish, such as this regal blue tang, live in coral reefs. The reefs provide them with protection.

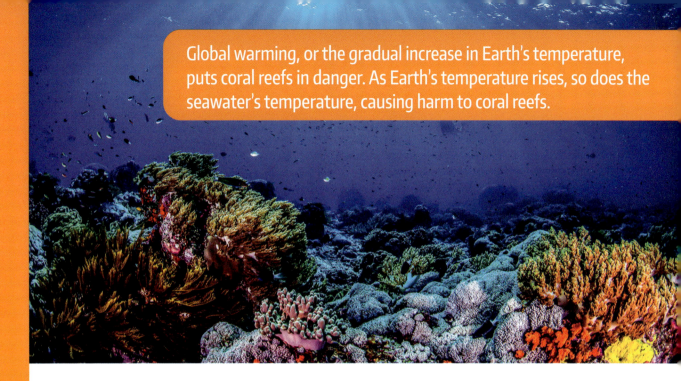

Global warming, or the gradual increase in Earth's temperature, puts coral reefs in danger. As Earth's temperature rises, so does the seawater's temperature, causing harm to coral reefs.

Corals have a skeleton that may be outside or inside the body. Stony corals have a hard, outside skeleton made of a mineral called calcium carbonate.

Corals produce eggs that develop into tiny creatures called planulae. Planulae develop into polyps. Corals also reproduce by budding. A bud is a new polyp that develops on the body of an old polyp. Some corals can live for up to 5,000 years, making them the longest-living animals on Earth.

Consider This
Coral reefs are often referred to as "rain forests of the sea." What similarities might exist between coral reefs and rain forests?

Flowery Animals

Though they can look like flowers, sea anemones are animals. Their "petals" are their tentacles. Like jellyfish and corals, sea anemones use their tentacles to catch their food. They eat shrimp, fish, and other small animals. Their tentacles may be red, yellow, green, blue, orange, brown, white, or a mix of colors. There are more than 1,000 species of sea anemones.

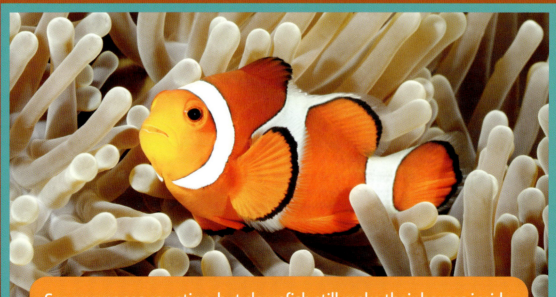

Sea anemones can sting, but clownfish still make their homes inside their tentacles! Clownfish have a protective layer of mucus that covers their body and keeps them safe from the stinger's toxins.

Sea anemones may live for over 100 years. Some live in groups.

Sea anemones have a soft body that may be thick and short or long and slender. Most of their body is made up of water. Sea anemones range from less than an inch (2.5 cm) to about 5 feet (1.5 m) across.

Most sea anemones rarely move. Some glide slowly or do slow somersaults. Sea anemones are usually attached to a hard surface like a rock, a seashell, or the back of a crab. Sometimes they float near the ocean's surface, or they might burrow into sand or mud.

Consider This

Young hermit crabs often pick up a young sea anemone to attach to their shell, and they become partners for life. Why might a hermit crab do this?

Hollow and Spiny Stars

Sea stars, also known as starfish, are not fish. They usually have five arms and are shaped like stars. There are about 1,800 species of sea stars. They come in many different colors. Most sea stars are 8 to 12 inches (20 to 30 cm) across.

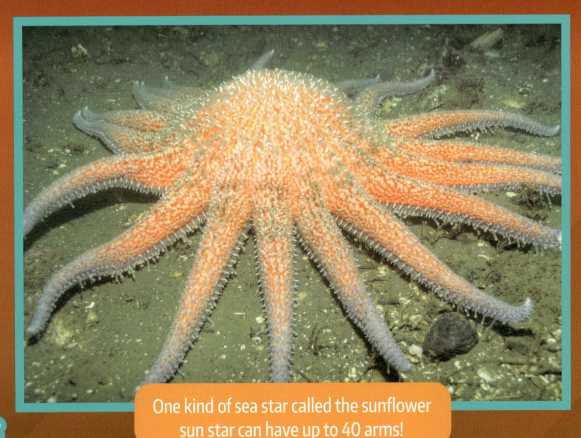

One kind of sea star called the sunflower sun star can have up to 40 arms!

Not all sea stars are perfectly star shaped. One sea star, the cushion starfish, has a rounder shape than other kinds.

Sea stars' arms are hollow and covered with spines. Many sea stars can grow another arm if they lose one. Sea stars move using hundreds of tube feet on their underside. In most sea stars, each tube foot has a suction cup on the end.

Most sea stars eat clams, oysters, and snails. They use their tube feet to pull apart the shells of larger prey. Some sea stars sweep food into their mouth. Others turn their stomach outward to take in their prey. Others can even swallow their prey whole.

Consider This
How would a sea star's ability to regrow an arm help it survive predator attacks?

Echinoderm Invertebrate

One group of marine invertebrates is called the **echinoderms**, and sea urchins belong to this group. Sea urchins look like globe-shaped pincushions. They are covered with long, movable spines that help the slow-moving animal "walk" and keep away enemies.

Sea urchins live in all seas except those of the polar regions. They are found on the ocean floor, usually on hard surfaces.

Sea urchins are usually red or purple. Some are less than an inch (2.5 cm) from side to side, while others measure 7 inches (18 cm) across. The spines of some sea urchins can be up to 12 inches (30 cm) long.

The word "urchin" comes from an old word for "hedgehog," and both sea urchins and hedgehogs have spikes on their bodies!

Some people eat the insides of sea urchins, which are called uni. Uni is often served raw in Japanese restaurants.

Sea urchins have an internal skeleton called a test. Their spines stick out of the test. These spines may be poisonous.

Sea urchins have tube feet, just like sea stars. The tube feet help the sea urchin grab food and bring it into its mouth. Their diet consists of mostly plant materials and other invertebrates.

WORD WISE
ECHINODERMS ARE A GROUP OF MARINE INVERTEBRATES THAT INCLUDE SEA STARS, SEA CUCUMBERS, AND SEA URCHINS. THEY HAVE SPINY, BUMPY SKIN THAT PROTECTS THEIR BODY.

Soft-Bodied Sponge

Sponges are unique creatures. They do not have the body parts most animals have. They don't even move around. Instead sponges stay attached to a rock or coral reef. For a long time, people thought sponges were plants. Scientists discovered that sponges are animals after watching them eat food by drawing it into their body.

Sponges can change the shape of their body. Most cells in their body can move around, and a few of them can even change from one type of cell to another.

Sponges filter large amounts of water through their body every day—around 20,000 times their own volume!

There are nearly 5,000 different species of sponges. Most live in the ocean, but some live in fresh water. Sponges come in a variety of shapes and sizes and colors. They can be as small as a bean or as large as a person. Sponges can be smooth and mushy or hard and prickly.

A sponge's body is a soft mass of cells supported by a skeleton. Holes in a sponge's skin let water flow inside. The water provides it with food and oxygen.

Consider This

Sponges attach to large surfaces like rocks and coral reefs. What other invertebrates do this? Why do you think this happens?

Invertebrate with Claws

Another type of marine invertebrate is called a **crustacean**. This group includes crabs. There are about 4,500 species of crabs. Crabs can be found in all oceans and in fresh water. Some crabs live on land too. Crabs have a hard covering known as an exoskeleton. They have five pairs of legs. The first pair has large pinching claws that help crabs eat and protect themselves. The tail of a crab is curled under its body.

Crabs have been on Earth for around 200 million years. That means they outlived dinosaurs!

Pea crabs spend most of their lives inside the shells of other animals, such as oysters, and often live in pairs.

Crabs come in a great range of sizes. Pea crabs may measure less than an inch (2.5 cm) across. The Japanese spider crab, on the other hand, can grow to be more than 1 foot (30 cm) across its body and measure 12 feet (4 m) with outstretched legs.

WORD WISE
CRUSTACEANS ARE AQUATIC INVERTEBRATES THAT HAVE EXOSKELETONS AND TWO PAIRS OF ANTENNAE. SOME EXAMPLES OF CRUSTACEANS ARE LOBSTERS, SHRIMP, KRILL, AND CRABS.

Most crabs feed on dead or decaying material. Some crabs may eat vegetable matter. Others eat small living animals. A crab's two large eyes extend from the head on movable stalks located above two pairs of antennae. The mouth is on the underside of the head.

All female crabs must lay their eggs in the water, even land crabs. The eggs are carried on the female's body until they hatch. Although some baby crabs leave the egg looking like small adults, most do not. Instead, a newly hatched crab is usually a tiny, see-through, legless creature that swims at the top of the water. At this stage the animal is called a zoea. Crabs then go through a process called metamorphosis. During this time, they molt—or shed their outside covering—many times. After metamorphosis, crabs are adults.

A female red crab can lay up to 100,000 eggs, which she keeps in a sac in her body before releasing them.

compare and contrast

Crustaceans have a hard exoskeleton, but they are still considered invertebrates. What characteristics do crustaceans have that make them invertebrates? How are they different from vertebrates?

Male fiddler crabs have one large claw and one smaller claw. They get the name "fiddler" because it looks like they're playing the fiddle!

Why Are Invertebrates Important?

Sea invertebrates are found all over the world in a variety of shapes, colors, and sizes. Some have tentacles, while others have spines or claws. One important similarity between them—besides their lack of a backbone—is that they each help keep their ecosystems balanced. For an ecosystem to be balanced, every animal that's a part of it plays a special, unique role.

Every animal on Earth plays a role in different food chains. Animals can be prey for other animals, predators to other animals, or both.

Pollution and global warming are threatening sea invertebrates' ability to survive. Toxic, warm waters can cause the organisms that live in them to die. It can also affect the food available to the organisms, which means they may starve.

Overfishing is also a threat to sea invertebrates. When people take too many of them, the sea invertebrates can't reproduce at the same rate and, as a result, begin to die off. Some countries restrict the amount of sea invertebrates, such as lobsters, crabs, and sea urchins, that people can fish at a time.

There are many groups dedicated to conserving and protecting sea invertebrates and other sea animals. They spread the word about the dangers these creatures face and try to change government policies to help keep the animals safe. It is crucial that we continue finding ways to protect sea invertebrates so they can live on Earth for many years to come.

Consider This

Without sea invertebrates, the ecosystems they're a part of would become unbalanced. What would happen to these ecosystems if sea invertebrates were gone?

Glossary

calcium carbonate A solid substance found in nature as limestone and marble and in plant ashes, bones, and shells and used especially in making lime and cement.

complex Having many different and connected parts.

ecosystem A system made up of a community of living things interacting with their environment especially under natural conditions.

metamorphosis The change in the form and habits of some animals from a young stage (as a tadpole or a caterpillar) to an adult stage (as a frog or a butterfly).

mollusk A member of a large group of invertebrate animals (such as snails, clams, and octopuses) with a soft body lacking segments and usually enclosed in a shell containing calcium.

mucus A sticky, slimy substance produced by the body.

navigation Being able to determine where a location is and plan a route to it.

paralyze To make something unable to act, function, or move.

pollution The action or process of making land, water, or air dirty and not safe or suitable to use.

spine A stiff, pointed, usually sharp, projecting part of a plant or animal. Also, sometimes a backbone.

tentacle A long flexible structure that sticks out usually around the head or mouth of an animal (as a jellyfish or sea anemone) and is used especially for feeling or grasping.

toxin A poisonous or venomous substance.

For More Information

Books

Gish, Melissa. *Spineless Sea Creatures.* Mankato, MN: Creative Education and Creative Paperbacks, 2019.

Zimmerman, Adeline J. *Sea Anemones.* Minneapolis, MN: Jump! Inc., 2022.

Zimmerman, Adeline J. *Sea Stars.* Minneapolis, MN: Jump! Inc., 2022.

Websites

English - Ocean Invertebrates - Sea Animals Without a Backbone - Annie Crawley
www.youtube.com/watch?v=5u-0Lrwa924
Watch a video about sea invertebrates to see your favorite creatures in action.

NASA Climate Kids: How Does Climate Change Affect the Ocean?
climatekids.nasa.gov/ocean/
Learn more about the deadly effects that global warming has on the ocean and the creatures that live there, as well as why the ocean is important for life on Earth.

Publisher's note to educators and parents: Our editors have carefully reviewed these websites to ensure that they are suitable for students. Many websites change frequently, however, and we cannot guarantee that a site's future contents will continue to meet our high standards of quality and educational value. Be advised that students should be closely supervised whenever they access the internet.

Index

C

clams, 6, 19
cnidarians, 10
coral, 14, 15, 16
crabs, 8, 17, 24, 25, 26, 27, 29
crustaceans, 24, 25, 27

E

echinoderms, 20
eggs, 9, 15, 26, 27
exoskeleton, 24, 25, 27

G

global warming, 15, 29

J

jellyfish, 10, 11, 12, 13, 16

K

krill, 25

L

lobsters, 8, 25, 29

M

mollusks, 6, 7,8
mouth, 12, 13, 14, 19, 21, 26

O

octopuses, 4, 5, 6, 7, 8, 9, 13
oysters, 6, 19, 25

P

poison/toxins, 13, 16, 21
polyp, 14, 15

R

reefs, 14, 15, 22, 23

S

sea anemones, 11, 16, 17
sea stars, 18, 19, 21
sea urchins, 20, 21, 29
shrimp, 16, 25
skeleton, 15, 21, 23
snails, 4, 19
spines, 19, 20, 21, 28
sponges, 4, 22, 23
squid, 6
stomach, 12, 19
suckers/suction cups, 7, 19

T

tentacles, 4, 6, 7, 11, 12, 13, 14, 16, 28